# GET THEM OVER IT!

## 57 TIPS FOR LEADERS TO HELP THEIR TEAMS EMBRACE THE DISCOMFORT OF CHANGE

*ONE A WEEK...PLUS A FEW. WE NEED ALL THE HELP WE CAN GET!*

ANNE BONNEY

Editor: Ken Wachsberger
Cover and Bio Page Photo: Michelle Laskowski Photography
Design for Cover/Interior: Kendra Cagle

ISBN: 978-0-578-89594-9

ANNE
BONNEY
*Ignite Your Influence*

YourChangeSpeaker.com

# Dedication

For all the leaders who just want
to get through this next change
without pulling out all their hair.

You've got this.

# TABLE OF
# CONTENTS

# THE
# INTRO

# CHANGE IS HARD.
## IT'S HARD FOR ANYONE.

But when you're a people leader, you get a double dose of challenge. You've got to deal with your own frustrations with change, AND you've got to deal with your team's challenges, resistance, attitude, grumpiness, fear, confusion, anger, and disruption to their normal productivity and achievement. Why did you take this job again?

In this book you'll find tips to help you move your teams through change. There are 57 so you have one for each week, and a few more. They're short, quick, and I tried to make them funny so you can quickly get some help moving your team through change and get a little stress relief at the same time. Keep it by your desk, and when leading your team gets overwhelming, grab it, open it, and read one tip; then get back to the fight. You'll find 4 big tips (Trust, Communicate, Resisters and Persevere) with sub-tips that follow it to give you more on that topic, so you can go right to the problem area for what you need.

And if you need some tips on dealing with the frustrations of change yourself, be sure to grab my first book, GET OVER IT!, which has similar quick tips to help you embrace the discomforts of change.

## You've got this. Now go give 'em heck
### (IN A NICE WAY)!

# BIG TIP

## #1

# FOUNDATION

## OF

# TRUST

"TRUST IS THE GLUE OF LIFE. IT'S THE MOST ESSENTIAL INGRE-
DIENT IN EFFECTIVE COMMUNICATION. IT'S THE FOUNDATIONAL
PRINCIPLE THAT HOLDS ALL RELATIONSHIPS."
—STEVEN COVEY

# A #1 KEY TO A HEALTHY
# WORK RELATIONSHIP IS TRUST.

As leaders, we have got to foster trust with and among our team members, especially if we want them to cheerfully skip alongside us through the change of the week. You want them to be able to relax and trust that you're giving them all the information they need, even when the full picture isn't available, so they don't have to kibitz at the water cooler trying to make up stories about what's going on. (They may do that anyway... Get over it!) If they're feeling confused, you want them to honestly believe that you'll give them what they need as soon as you can. If they don't like something, you want them to honestly believe that there is, nevertheless, a larger plan at play, being orchestrated by intelligent, professional people who are thinking it through. Boy, that would be nice. Wouldn't it?

Ideally, this trust building happens before you have to undergo any change, but let's face it, sometimes we're drop-kicked into the middle of a transition storm with an inside-out umbrella! But don't worry if you haven't had the chance to develop trust with the team you're leading through this change. You haven't got time to worry. Start today and the next bunch of tips will help.

*"Trust is built and maintained through
many small actions over time."*
— LOLLY DASKAL

## BE LIKE A
### *WINDOW...*

# BE
# TRANSPARENT

The main complaints I hear when I'm doing leadership and communication work-shops are "We never get enough information," and "We get information too late," and "The information we get is incomplete." Communication is so important, especially when it comes to building trust. Your team needs to know that you're giving them all the information that you have, or all the information that you can (because sometimes you can't spill all the beans when you have them).

**BE TRANSPARENT.** Be sure you're making an intentional effort to be honest with your team.

**OVERCOMMUNICATE,** so they trust that when they're confused, you're doing the best you can to give them all the information that you have.

When there are holes in the information, **ADMIT IT!** Tell them that you don't have it, but you'll give it to them as soon as you have it. If the information is likely to change, tell them that, too!

**BE HONEST,** especially when the info you have doesn't match the info they want.

TIP #3

# TALK
## ABOUT THE
# ELEPHANT

Change is hard, especially when you're in a large change that involves many people and many moving parts. Communication is hard and often doesn't happen well, or at all. (Let's be honest!) **Talk about the elephant in the room:** the fact that they're having to work harder these days to implement these changes. Admit that you don't have all the information or you can't share it because the plans aren't completely flushed out yet. Assure them you will do your best to make sure they have the full, true picture as soon as possible.

# BEING HONEST AND OPEN WITH YOUR TEAMS WILL GIVE THEM A LOT LESS TO COMPLAIN AND WORRY AND MAKE STUFF UP ABOUT.

IT ALSO MAKES YOU A LOT MORE ACCESSIBLE.

## TIP #4

# DON'T
## LEAVE THEM ON
# AN ISLAND

# ORGANIZATIONAL CHANGES REQUIRE YOUR TEAM TO OFTEN DRAMATICALLY CHANGE THE WAY THEY DO THINGS.

Computer system changes especially throw some people into full-blown panic. Any change that requires someone to do something they've been doing for a long time differently is scary! First of all, people may really like and be comfortable with the old way.

*Even when they're able to get beyond their preference for the old way, fear sets in. Nobody likes to fail.*

Fear of job security comes in *("Will I get fired if I can't do the new way as well as I did before?")* and fear of judgment as well *("If I'm the only one who can't catch on to this new computer system, people are going to think I'm an idiot!").* Be sure your team knows what training and post-training support they'll get to help them learn the new system. Be on the lookout for people who are struggling; partner them with someone who is catching on quickly and may be able to explain it in a way that solidifies it in the struggler's head. Give job aids if you can. Just be sure they know that they'll get support through the learning process, so they don't waste their time worrying about that.

# TIP #5

# FOLLOW
## THROUGH

*THIS IS A BIG ONE.*

# WHEN YOU SAY YOU'RE GOING TO DO SOMETHING, DO IT!

*IF YOU CAN'T DO IT, BE SURE TO EXPLAIN WHAT'S GOING ON.*

*(See Tip 2 about being like a window…transparent)*

If you're not going to be able to do something, don't say "I'll try" or "I'll look into that," because if they already trust you, they'll see that as an affirmative, while you're trying to be shifty. Just say, "That's not possible and here's why." Someone in one of my workshops once said, "I'd rather be sad than surprised." Have the courage to give them the real answer. They may not like it, and they'll probably gripe and scowl, but at least they'll know you're being truthful with them, and their trust in you won't be damaged.

# TIP #6

# HAVE THEIR BACK

Be sure your team knows you're going to support them through the whole process. When they need something, try to get it: extended deadlines, additional training support, supplies, more manpower, whatever. Sometimes satisfying their needs is not going to be possible, so be honest whether it is or not, but be sure to make an effort. When someone makes a mistake, don't make them stand out in the cold alone taking the heat. Be sure to take responsibility for how you could have helped them be more successful and commit to helping them learn and do better in the future.

## DON'T DEFLECT BLAME.
## STAND WITH YOUR TEAM AND FIX IT.

*AND WHEN THINGS GO RIGHT, YOU'D BETTER BE SINGING THE WHOLE TEAM'S PRAISES, BECAUSE THERE'S NO WAY YOU COULD BE DOING ALL THAT ALONE.*

# TIP #7

## BRING
## THE TEAM
## TOGETHER

I used to roll my eyes at team-building activities. Whether it was a simple potluck or a full-day, off-site retreat, I thought, "Can't we just get back to work?" Admittedly, I needed to lighten up, but I also wasn't fully appreciating the value of shared success, shared experience, and the opportunity to develop "The Poodle Bond."

# YOU SEE, WHEN WE INTERACT ON NON-WORK-RELATED TOPICS, WE LEARN ABOUT COMMONALITIES THAT WE HAVE WITH EACH OTHER.

*THAT HUMANIZES OTHERS AND WE REALIZE WE'RE ALIKE.*

*("You like Poodles? I GREW UP WITH POODLES! OH, MY GOODNESS, We're so alike!")* When we can see how we're alike, we're more likely to trust eachother, and act in a civil manner when the stuff hits the fan at work. So, facilitate opportunities for your team to build successes together, and simply get to know each other as humans. This will boost the trust factor and make it a lot easier to ask for help, admit mistakes, and fully capitalize on the open collaboration that will bring amazing results.

# Tip #8

# DON'T
## BE A
# STICK IN THE MUD

# JUST BECAUSE OUR WORK IS IMPORTANT AND SERIOUS DOESN'T MEAN WE CAN'T LAUGH, HAVE FUN, AND ENJOY OURSELVES AT WORK.

*People work better when they're engaged and enjoying themselves.*

They relax when they're laughing, and they're more likely to accept change as a result. When you laugh with someone, feel-good juices flow around in your brain, and you let your guard down, which builds trust. I'm not saying you spend the whole day clowning around, but encourage people to laugh, find perspective, and have fun. It will pay dividends when it comes to building and maintaining trust within your team.

# Tip #9

## CELEBRATE
## GOOD TIMES,
### COME ON!

# IF YOU WANT PEOPLE TO TRUST YOU AND YOUR TEAM, THEY NEED TO FEEL APPRECIATED.

They need to feel that their efforts don't go unnoticed. Be sure to take the time to celebrate wins. Maybe it's just a quick "Hey everyone, you worked your butts off on that project, and it made a huge difference. Thank you!" Or maybe you pull an Oprah, and everyone gets a new car! *(Or somewhere in between.)* Whatever the case, be sure to take the time to celebrate progress, completion, success, and effort!

Let's talk about this effort thing for a sec, because sometimes the best intentions combined with the hardest work still result in a crummy outcome. Be sure that the effort is appreciated, even if it didn't turn out as you wanted.

*People are going to beat themselves up plenty for not achieving success. Be sure you show appreciation for the effort and the intentions.*

Debrief on the learnings so you can all get better together. This is going to create a sense of trust so your team will give you their all, including when they're massively uncomfortable with a change...which is when you need them the most.

## Tip #10

# COMMUNICATE
# WINS

Sometimes your team won't see the successes resulting from their efforts. When a client sends positive feedback on the service they received, or the CEO recognizes a process innovation that someone on your team came up with, communicate that to your team. When a product that they helped create is selling like gangbusters, let them know!

# WHEN THERE'S A CALL OUT TO THE EFFORTS OF YOUR TEAM IN AN EXECUTIVE MEETING, TELL THEM!

*Communicate the wins, even if they're not exactly the main outcome.*

Sometimes people get blinded by the process and the main desired outcome, and they miss the little wins along the way. Be the one who points those out. Not only will your team know and trust that you see the good stuff they're creating, but they'll be more likely to see them and point them out to each other, creating a much more positive team culture, which is going to really come in handy when you get to the ugly depths of change.

TIP #11

# CREATE AN
## "ENVIRONMENT OF
# SAFE FAILURE"

In order for trust to be built, we need a level of psychological safety. We need to know that we're not going to be punished or judged if we put ourselves out there and take a risk.

# CHANGE REQUIRES A LOT OF BIG RISKS.
## Some of those big risks are:

- Trying a new way. *(I might suck at this!)*
- Saying, "I don't get it; I need help." *(They might laugh at me or judge me as an idiot.)*
- Saying, "I don't agree, and I have a really good business reason why and I want to tell you what it is in an emotionally mature manner." *(They might see me as a rebel dissenter trying to overthrow the administration.)*
- Saying, "I hate this. Could I please vent and ask some angry questions so I can understand this better and move towards getting over it?" *(I don't want to be a jerk, but this sucks!)*
- Sharing an idea that could make the whole thing easier/better/more efficient. *(They might laugh at my idea.)*

Our teams need to feel safe in taking those risks, so we need to accept, even encourage new ideas. Take the time to listen to people and encourage them to share. Create agreements with your team on how you're going to deal with conflict and how you'll conduct yourselves in meetings and hold each other accountable for those standards. Be sure people feel respected and valued, and trust will skyrocket.

# TIP #12

## SHARE
## THE
## GLORY

# BE SURE THAT CREDIT IS GIVEN WHERE IT IS DUE.

If something was a team effort, be sure the team gets credit. If someone worked hard on something, be sure they're recognized. If someone calls you out for something someone else should also get the credit for, make a point that they get it. If your team thinks you're getting all the glory from the higher ups for all of their effort, trust is going to go in the trash can. Be sure the team and the individuals on the team are getting the visibility for their efforts. It will make you look good, because you're their leader!

(HOPEFULLY YOU'RE DOING OTHER GOOD THINGS, TOO!)

# TIP #13

## BE
# HANDY
## (NOT HAND-SY THAT'S DIFFERENT!)

Have you ever had a boss who glorifies their "open door policy" but their door is always closed *(figuratively and literally)*? If you want your team to trust you, you've got to be available for questions, ideas, challenges, support, and feedback. This means two things:

1. You're physically around, and the door is actually open, so they have access to you.
2. You're emotionally available. You accept ideas, you're a great listener, and you make people feel valued and respected.

## I KNOW WHAT YOU'RE THINKING:
### IF I MAKE MYSELF AVAILABLE TO EVERYONE, I'LL NEVER GET A SECOND TO MYSELF!

YES! You need to protect your own time. The way I like to deal with this issue is to tell my team, "I want to be available for you so you can share your challenges, your ideas, and your thoughts, but I also have a TON on my plate to get done, just like you do. If my door is closed, please, unless a bone is sticking out of your arm, don't come in. You can email or IM me for availability, but assume I'm occupied. When the door is open, I am available, come on in, I'm all yours." Then, I make sure that I only close my door when I'm really needing to be left alone. For a significant portion of my day, my team is going to find my door open, so they can trust that I'm not sitting in my office with my feet up taking a Cosmo quiz and eating bon bons when my door is closed. Same goes for virtual interactions. Make the rule, respect the rule for others, and enforce it. They'll catch on, and appreciate it going forward.

# TIP #14

# CONFESS
## YOUR
# FOIBLES

# IF YOU MESS UP, FESS UP!

## BELIEVE ME, THEY ALREADY KNOW.

If you don't admit it, they're probably already talking about it anyway. Admitting your mistakes not only disarms them, but it gives you the opportunity to show strength in how you're going to fix them and learn from them in the future. This is a fabulous role model behavior, but it also creates a culture where mistakes and failure aren't huge, dramatic, terrible, career-ending disasters. It creates an environment where the risks that come with change are less scary, and trust will continue to rise.

# TIP #15

## ROLL UP YOUR
## SLEEVES,
## CHARLIE!

# BE SURE YOUR TEAMS SEE THAT YOU'RE WORKING, TOO.

## ROLL UP YOUR SLEEVES AND LEAD FROM THE FRONT, NOT IN THE EASY CHAIR OF MANAGEMENT.

When the department is in a crunch time, your team needs to see you crunching with them. If you want them to give their all, they need to believe you're giving your all. I'm not talking about words. Don't tell them how much you're doing. They need to see you working, understand your contribution as well. Sometimes it means pitching in and doing their work alongside them to be sure everything gets done by the deadline. Other times you'll have different tasks to achieve the goal. Whatever the case, if they trust that you're busting your butt, they're more likely to bust theirs, too. Don't be secretive about what you're doing and be sure you're in there getting your hands dirty with them. Sometimes it means longer hours, but the investment in trust will pay dividends in the long run.

BIG TIP

#16

# COMMUNICATE

*"Motivate players through communication, being
honest with them, having them respect and appreciate
your ability and your help."*

—TOMMY LASORDA

In all of the seminars I've led over the years, I've had many conversations about effective and ineffective leadership in change and no one ever says...

*"YA' KNOW, THEY JUST COMMUNICATE TOO MUCH. WE GET ENTIRELY TOO MUCH INFORMATION."*

## THAT NEVER HAPPENS.

More often I hear complaints about the amount of information (*too little*), the timeliness of the information (*too late or after the other teams*), or the completeness and clarity and consistency of the information (*or lack thereof*). Communication is so important. Your team needs to have the information in order to execute the change, but also, when there actually isn't a complete set of information, they need to be able to think, "Ok, I don't know what's going on, but they always tell me as soon as they can, so I'm going to relax and just do the best I can until the information is available. I trust they'll give it." Hopefully they don't have to say that very often, but that kind of amazing epiphany comes only within a culture of complete communication!

*The next 16 tips can be like a check list of information to be sure you're communicating.*

# Tip #17

## WHEN
### IS THIS
# HAPPENING?

# WHEN IS THIS ALL HAPPENING?

## WHAT DOES OUR TIMELINE LOOK LIKE?

Learning and implementing a new computer system in a week is completely different than doing it in four months. People often assume the worst, so be sure to communicate when it's all going down, so they don't freak out. *(Or they do freak out, but because of reality and not assumed urgency!)* Also let them know phases if that's relevant. The more information they have on how much the timeline has been developed, the more they're going to see the path to the end of the change, and trust that the people in charge have everything under control.

Tip #18

# CLARIFY
## EXPECTATIONS

# BE SURE TO CLARIFY PEOPLE'S ROLES IN A CHANGE, AND WHAT THEY'RE EXPECTED TO MAINTAIN OR TAKE ON IN THE PROCESS.

Sometimes, when someone is resisting, you also need to have a tough but respectful and tactful conversation around your expectations of the way they handle the challenges associated with the change. You can be understanding and yet firm in communicating that you expect them to get on board and support the organization through this change, as that is their job. Again, solicit their input, listen to their concerns, offer help and support. But also, be clear that you expect them to get on board.

*SOMETIMES HEARING THAT BLUNT REMINDER IS WHAT WILL SNAP SOMEONE OUT OF THEIR FUNK ... SOMETIMES.*

# Tip #19

## WITH A
# LITTLE HELP
## FROM MY FRIENDS

When people are surprised and scared about a change, and aren't confident in their ability to learn a new process or system, that fear manifests as an assumption that they're going to be dropped into the fire and left to figure it all out for themselves.

## BE SURE THEY KNOW WHAT KIND OF SUPPORT THEY'RE GOING TO GET.

What training? What kind of post-training support? Will there be extra help with the day-to day while they're executing the change. Are they going to be expected to train the new boss? Be sure to communicate what they are and are not going to get, and, again, don't ignore holes in the support. If there's something you know they'd like, or that would really help, but for whatever reason you are unable to provide that, talk about it. Let them know that you know it would be helpful, but here's the reason we're not going to be able to do it. If you talk about it, they still may be resentful and resistant, but at least they won't accuse you of not seeing the need.

# TIP #20

## WHAT
## TRAINING
## IS
## AVAILABLE?

# WHEN IT COMES TO A CHANGE THAT INVOLVES LEARNING SOMETHING NEW, BE SURE YOU COMMUNICATE WHAT TRAINING THEY'RE GOING TO GET AND WHEN.

Be specific, because the fear of failure comes in like a wrecking ball, especially for those people who didn't have a great experience with school, or who have been in the same job for a long time. If no formal training program is available, but there are some optional trainings they could take, be sure they know about them. Like, when someone is being moved to a leadership or supervisory position. That change, while positive because they may be getting a promotion, is also scary, because they're being asked to do a new and different job. Maybe your company doesn't offer an official supervisor training program, but you do have a leadership training program available to everyone. Be sure that information is communicated so they know the resources available. Maybe it's not an internal training, but professional development funds are available that they can use for outside training.

*BAM! COMMUNICATE THAT!*

TIP #21

# ASK
## THEM

# THE BEST WAY TO COMMUNICATE EXACTLY WHAT YOUR TEAM NEEDS COMMUNICATED IS TO ASK THEM!

*WHAT DO YOU WANT TO KNOW? WHAT DO YOU NEED? WHAT QUESTIONS DO YOU HAVE? WHAT RUMORS ARE YOU HEARING? ASK THEM!*

If you have regular check-ins, you'll keep that line of communication open, and your team will be more likely to tell you what they need, which means they think you're accessible and that means they trust you! Solicit from them what they need. You may not be able to accommodate their every request, but at least you're listening, and you might be able to provide something that is similar, a little less but still helpful, or something seemingly different that still solves the problem they're trying to solve. They may ask for a raise *(ok, they'll always ask for a raise!)* that you may not be able to give, but learning that they may want to pursue a higher degree could lead to your recommendation that professional development funds be made available to them, in essence giving them a raise through other benefits the company will pay for. Be sure you know what employee assistance your HR department has available because that could really help your people out!

# TIP #22

# LET 'EM VENT

# I DON'T KNOW ABOUT YOU, BUT SOMETIMES I JUST NEED TO LET IT ALL OUT.

*I JUST NEED TO SHARE WHAT I HATE ABOUT A SITUATION AND RELEASE THE BEAST.*

Once I've had a chance to do that, I feel better, and I can get on with getting over it! Any time a big change was announced in a company I worked for, I would pull my team together right after it and say, "ok, COMPLAIN! What do you hate about this? What scares you? What angers you? What do you think the challenges are going to be?" I gave them a chance to complain in a constructive way *(because you know they're going to, one way or another!)*. They get it out, and you learn where they stand, and might just learn about a challenge or problem that you hadn't considered. Give them a time limit, because some people can take complaining to epic proportions, but do give them maybe a little more time than you'd like to. That time together also gives you a chance to do some team problem solving to start moving the conversation into the future so you can all move forward together, having discussed the elephant in the room.

*(THEY'LL STILL COMPLAIN AT THE WATER COOLER, BUT IT WILL BE MUCH LESS TOXIC.)*

# TIP #23

## SHUT UP
### AND
# LISTEN!

# WE ALL WANT TO BE LISTENED TO.

*It's a way people feel respected,
and a great way to show that we care
about the information they have to share,
and we care about them as humans.*

As a leader, the best skill you can hone is your ability to listen. I don't mean you're going to give hours of your time to someone, because you've got a lot to do, too. I'm saying that when you do give someone your time, even if it's just five minutes, be fully present and listen to understand. Don't start planning what you're going to say next *(or what you're going to have for dinner)*. Listen and paraphrase so your team member really feels heard and respected. You can also spot assumptions and mis-understandings that, if you can clear them up, might just get them over it! So, learn how to listen. It takes time and patience, but it's a huge investment in building trust, and your team moving forward past resistance.

# TIP #24

## COMMUNICATE
# CHANGES
## ASAP

# WHEN SOMETHING IS CHANGING, OFTEN A RIPPLE EFFECT OCCURS, FURTHER SHIFTING THE SANDS UNDER YOUR TEAM'S FEET.

When you're in a season of large change, and your team is already unsettled, be sure you're communicating additional smaller changes as soon as you can. It's really tough to learn about decisions that impact you from another team, or, worse, from a customer or the news or an advertisement. Trust is going to take a massive hit, and your team will start freaking out that they're not getting the information they need. Even if you don't think they need the information.

*IF IT IMPACTS THEM, COMMUNICATE IT!*

This is a great time to make a central hub of information, like an intranet scrolling newsfeed, or updates on the front page so people have somewhere to look for up-to-the-second information. Then all you have to do is remind them to make a habit of checking there. It's better coming out of your mouth but getting the information ANY way is better than not getting it at all.

# Tip #25

## APPRECIATE
## APPRECIATE
# APPRECIATE!

In late 2002, I was a customer service representative at Under Armour, selling tight t-shirts over the phone to Billy's mom in DesMoines. One day I got to work and on my desk was a small notecard that read,

ANNE,

YOUR ENERGY AND ENTHUSIASM ARE APPRECIATED THROUGHOUT THE OFFICE. THANK YOU!

— KEVIN PLANK

I don't know if I got a raise or a bonus that year. I probably got a few free t-shirts, but all these years later, I'm still talking about that note. A simple thank you! It made me feel valued, respected and seen. Especially during a time of change, thanking someone for dealing with the challenge, for taking on the learning, or helping to make it a success will go far in motivating them to keep going. NEVER underestimate the value of appreciation.

## OK, NOW READ THIS PAGE AGAIN.
THANK YOU

# TIP #26

## PAINT
## THE
# LIGHTHOUSE

# OFTEN CHANGE TAKES A LONG TIME, AND IT'S EXHAUSTING.

*New frustrations crop up without warning. Tempers wear thin.*

Be sure your team has a vision of what success looks like, and how the business will be better once the change is complete. Give them a lighthouse, so when they're ripping their hair out, they can see the benefit of perseverance. Having that vision will help them stay the course and work through their frustrations while continuing to move your business forward.

# TIP #27

## WHY THE HECK
## ARE WE
# DOING THIS?

# ORGANIZATIONAL CHANGE ISN'T ALWAYS LOGICAL TO EVERYONE WHO IS IMPACTED BY IT.

They don't always understand the reasons for the change, but adults always want to know why, especially when the change is creating discomfort for them. Positive change also isn't always positive for everyone involved. A procedural change may give the client easier access to the information they need but be a more burdensome process for your team. Be sure they understand why a change is being made.

YES, HELPING PEOPLE UNDERSTAND WHY A CHANGE IS NECESSARY MAY TAKE A LITTLE LONGER, BUT IT WILL HELP THEM UNDERSTAND THE WHOLE PUZZLE WHEN THEIR PARTICULAR PIECE IS FEELING PRETTY AWFUL.

Another WHY that can be helpful is why things can't stay the way they are. Calling the old way into question will help those who are strongly resistant to the change to understand how their beloved old way just isn't ok anymore.

# GIVE THEM THE
# LONG VISION
## AND THE
## SHORT-TERM PLAYS

When a big change is being made, people will often balk and completely resist because looking at the end result from where they are seems insurmountable. It's like telling someone who has never run a mile that they're going to run a marathon. If I'm afraid of even running one, 26.2 is an impossibility. But if we say, "In a year we'll run 26.2 miles, but first, let's focus on running three miles. Once we know we can run three, we can go for five. Then once that's possible, let's tackle eight miles. Then 10, then 13. Our confidence builds until eventually 26 doesn't seem so bad!"

SAME AT WORK

# BE SURE PEOPLE UNDERSTAND THE ULTIMATE GOAL, BUT ALSO GIVE THEM THE SHORTER-TERM GOALS TO FOCUS THEIR ENERGY ON RIGHT NOW.

For today, don't worry about the end result. If we hop on these short-term goals, we'll eventually mount the unsurmountable!

# TIP #29

# BE POSITIVE,
### BUT
## But Not
## Too Much!

# "I'D RATHER BE SAD THAN SURPRISED."

I heard this from a leader at a communication workshop I once led, and it stuck with me. We talk about being positive, but that doesn't mean don't be honest. If a change implementation is going to suck, let your team know that. Set a realistic expectation up front so they don't feel like you duped them. Your positivity can come in your belief in the team and their ability to conquer the challenge. It may come in the support, training, and pizza you're going to provide to get them through.

*(This is a good time to pop forward and read Tip #43: Feed them!)*

Don't drown in the horror of the upcoming change, but don't sugar coat it either. Don't sell them a bag of goods if they're getting a pile of…well, you know. Be honest. Give them the straight story so you don't lose trust, and they know what to expect going into it. Hopefully they'll be pleasantly surprised when it isn't that bad.

# TIP #30

## YOU'VE COME A
# LONG WAY
## BABY!

# SOMETIMES WE GET SO FOCUSED ON THE END GOAL, THAT WE FORGET TO LOOK BACK AND SEE HOW FAR WE'VE COME.

Be sure to communicate and celebrate the progress your team is making. Remind them to look back and see how much they've accomplished. When they still have a long way to go, and could get discouraged, this will give them a boost of forward momentum. I have to do this with my own business. I'm so busy charging towards the next goal, and looking at what still needs to be done, that I lose sight of how much I've truly done and accomplished.

*Point this stuff out to your team. It really helps morale!*

TIP #31

# SOLICIT
## THEIR
# INPUT

Some people will give you more feedback and ask more questions than you know what to do with. Others aren't comfortable speaking up for fear that someone will reject their idea, judge them as a whiner, or think they're an idiot for not knowing. Be sure you're creating a forum for everyone to share. When I worked with Les Mills, and they announced a huge organizational change, I pulled my whole team together for a venting meeting! I told them to complain, to ask their questions, to share their challenges. I gave them an appropriate forum to speak up. Since I'd built a foundation of trust with them, they knew they would be heard. Even with that foundation in place, I knew that some people still wouldn't be comfortable sharing, or would need time to process what they'd heard, so I followed up with an anonymous survey. I shared that their input was valuable because they had a unique perspective on the change and how it would impact their job and our clients, and I needed to know what it was so we could consider all potential roadblocks.

## SEEK THIS INFORMATION OUT BECAUSE IT'LL LET YOU KNOW WHERE YOUR TEAM IS. IT'LL HELP WITH THEIR MOTIVATION AND ENGAGEMENT BECAUSE THEY'LL FEEL HEARD.

AND YOU JUST MIGHT LEARN SOMETHING VALUABLE!

# TIP #32

## TEACH THEM
## TO HAVE TOUGH
# CONVERSATIONS

When we announced the new reporting system that would give organization-wide visibility over our staffing situation, one veteran director balked. She liked her old way of keeping track, she didn't trust that our company could build the system I was so excited about, and she was downright angry about the disruption to her routine. After I announced the change, she sat with arms crossed, fuming. She didn't say a word in the meeting, then yelled at me in my office after. She was angry and scared and frustrated and had also never learned how to express her fears and frustrations in a respectful and tactful way. I was asking them to share feedback and challenges, but they didn't have the communication skills to be able to do that in a constructive way, which led to either a blow up or a bottle up *(which is accompanied by negative/ disgruntled gossip!)*. Have a lunch-and-learn to teach your team how to give feedback in a non-defensive, non-emotional way. Pass around an article and discuss it. Share a video they can watch or recommend a book or podcast to listen to, or bring in a professional trainer.

## GIVE THEM THE SKILLS THEY NEED TO BE ABLE TO EFFECTIVELY SHARE WHAT'S BUGGING THEM...

and deal with conflict so it can turn into a constructive sharing of information and perspectives rather than a relationship-damaging mess.

# #33

# RESISTERS

*"PEOPLE DON'T RESIST CHANGE. THEY RESIST BEING CHANGED."*
—PETER SENGE

# CHANGE IS HARD FOR MOST PEOPLE, BUT IT'S ESPECIALLY HARD FOR SOME.

Whether they need to see the whole path before proceeding *(which, with change, is highly unlikely)*, they bear scars from a past poorly managed change, or they lack trust in the organization or the individuals in charge of the change, some people dig their heels in and simply refuse to get on board. Having the skills to help these individuals through the change is helpful, but, most importantly, you need patience! Good luck with that!

**Oh, and please note:** It's unlikely that these tips will result in immediate and dramatic change.

THIS IS HUMAN INTERACTION, NOT MAGIC!

But, with trust, communication, and these next seven tips implemented consistently over time, you have the best chance at success with your toughest characters, so settle in, and keep going!

# TIP #34

## ASK THEM

# WHAT'S UP!

When you know someone is having trouble with a change, either openly resisting or passive-aggressively sabotaging it behind your back (that's always fun!), many leaders will ignore it, thinking, "They'll get over it in time." Unfortunately, that approach can extend the resistance and increase negative feelings towards your leadership, the project and the organization. Instead, have a conversation with them. Name their emotions by saying, "I can see that you're frustrated with the change we have going on. I'd like to know more about what challenges, fears, and frustrations you have with it so I can help ease the transition." ASK! Just simply ASK, "What's up?" Not in a "What the heck is wrong with you?" kind of way. Ask with a genuine curiosity to understand their point of view. What you learn will help you lead them through the change, and it might give you insights to where communication is breaking down, or why others are resisting.

## OPEN THE DANCE FLOOR FOR A CONVERSATION AROUND THEIR CHALLENGE.

AT THE VERY LEAST, THEY FEEL HEARD, WHICH MAY BE JUST WHAT THEY NEED TO GET OVER IT AND GET ON WITH IT.

# TIP #35

## PUT ON
## THEIR
## SHOES

# People who resist may get on your last nerve.

You want to just get the job done, and they're standing, firm and flat-footed right in your way. Often this interference robs us of our ability (or desire) to empathize, but as an emotionally intelligent leader, you need to be able to interact with everyone on your team in a respectful and professional way. Doing this gets a lot easier when you're able to put yourself in someone's shoes and see where they're coming from. Maybe they had a horrible experience with change in the past. Maybe they did really poorly in school, and the prospect of spending two weeks in class to thoroughly understand the new computer system is terrifying and depressing for them.

## APPRECIATING WHERE THEY'RE COMING FROM WILL HELP YOU ASSUAGE THEIR FEARS, APPRECIATE THEIR EFFORTS, AND HAVE MORE PATIENCE.

It doesn't mean that it's acceptable for them to openly resist and not do their job, but it will give you a little more patience and understanding as you work through their resistance.

# TIP #36

## DON'T
### GO DOWN
# WITH THEM

# EMPATHY IS GOOD.

## SYMPATHY ISN'T HELPFUL!

Sympathizing means you not only put yourself in their shoes, but you take on their feelings, go down there with them, and validate their behavior as a result of their feelings. Appreciate and acknowledge their feelings but share your confidence that they'll be able to get through this change in a positive and calm way. Ask for, help shape, and expect their behavior to reflect their commitment to make the change a success.

# TIP #37

# CONNECT THEM
## WITH AN
# ADAPTOR

# HAVE YOU EVER SAID SOMETHING TO YOUR CHILDREN, AN IMPORTANT LESSON, MAYBE OVER AND OVER, AND THEY JUST DIDN'T LISTEN?

Then some basketball player, friend's mom, or teacher says the exact same thing and they act like it's the most brilliant, most novel thing they've ever heard?

YEAH.

Sometimes because of our role, our tone, our history with that person, or the way we say something, it just might not sink in. When you're dealing with a hard-core change resister, suggest they connect with someone who is making the change work, or who has made it work in the past. Maybe they'll be able to help them get over it more effectively than you will.

# TIP #38

## GIVE THEM
### THE
# TOUGH INFO

# WE CAN BE EMPATHETIC, UNDERSTANDING, GIVE THEM TIME, AND SOME PEOPLE JUST AREN'T GOING TO COME AROUND.

They dig in their heels so hard they dig a moat around your desk. It may be time for a tactful and respectful conversation that includes the possible negative consequences of not getting on board. Whether it's progressive discipline based on the organizations HR policies, removal from the job or project team, not earning the bonus as laid out, or whatever, sometimes people need a little pain to change behavior. Obviously discuss your options with HR first, and be sure you educate yourself on how to have tough conversations well.

*THAT SAID, HAVE THE COURAGE TO HAVE THE TOUGH CONVERSATION.*

You're not threatening them. You've giving them the whole picture. At the end of the day, the resistor is going to make their own decision on what they're going to do, so give them all the information they need to make the best decision possible for themselves.

# TIP #39

# SHOW THEM
## THE
# BENEFITS

*Let's face it.*

# NONE OF US ARE SITTING AROUND LOOKING FOR WORK TO DO.

When you add change management to the already jam-packed hustle and bustle, we're stretched thin. As a result, we often don't give a full picture to our teams about the benefits of the change. If we just say, "Here's what we're doing. Go!" and they don't understand the reasons or the bigger picture, they're much less likely to jump on board, take initiative, and be the change ninjas that we need.

A few years ago, in a change management seminar I was leading, a manager said to me, "I'm paying them to do their jobs. I shouldn't have to sell it to them." Sure, that's one way to look at it, and. yes, that approach may get reluctant compliance, but it will not give them ownership and empowerment. Taking the extra time to explain the reasons and benefits of the change *(or perhaps why the old way won't work anymore)* will help people see the necessity. Even when they're inconvenienced and uncomfortable, they will know the why, and their compliance will be much more positive as will their long-term engagement and retention.

# TIP #40

# GIVE 'EM
# TIME

# SOMETIMES PEOPLE JUST NEED TO BE HEARD.

THEN THEY NEED A HOT SECOND TO GET OVER IT. IF POSSIBLE, LET THEM GRUMBLE. LET THEM RESIST. DON'T EXPECT IMMEDIATE TURNAROUND.

Obviously you're not going to let that drag on for a year and a half, but maybe give them a little more time than you'd like to, because that might be all they need to get over it and get on with it.

And if they're just grumbling, but they're making it work, acknowledge the effort both to yourself and to them. They might have a sourpuss attitude for a while, but actually be taking the right action. Be on the lookout for that. If their grouchy moaning is the worst of your problems, count yourself lucky!

BIG TIP

#41

# PERSEVERE

ALL THE WAY TO THE

*NEW NORMAL*

"WE CAN DO ANYTHING WE WANT TO DO IF
WE STICK TO IT LONG ENOUGH."
—HELEN KELLER

# AN INITIAL CHANGE ANNOUNCEMENT IS OFTEN MET WITH LOUD RESISTANCE, FRUSTRATION, AND BACKLASH.

*Once everyone calms down, it's time to get to the execution, which, depending on the change, could take a while.*

It's similar to the pioneers in the 1800s United States leaving the coastal cities to find their own land and a new life. Along the way they needed to cross mountains, and deal with weather, illness, broken wheels, and wildlife that was as hungry as they were. Similar to leaving the comfort of the old familiar way of life and trying a new path, it takes a while to get to the point where the change becomes comfortable again. We need to continue supporting our people after the initial push, to keep their morale up and productivity strong.

# TIP #42

## SHRINK

### THE

# ELEPHANT

# ANY TIME SOMEONE FEELS CHALLENGED, THEY BECOME UNCOMFORTABLE, AND WE HUMANS ALWAYS WANT TO GET BACK TO BEING COMFORTABLE ASAP.

People sometimes think they're alone in their discomfort and fear, and it has an isolating impact, so talk about it!

### Normalize it.

Acknowledge it and thank the team for their efforts and continued slogging to the new normal. Give them an appropriate forum to talk about their discomfort and bond over it, and you'll have a much more positive and supportive culture throughout the team.

# TIP #43

# FEED
## THEM

# YOU THINK I'M KIDDING. I'M NOT!

FOOD RELEASES THE FEEL-GOOD ENDORPHINS IN YOUR BRAIN, SO IF YOU WANT TO IMPROVE MORALE DURING THE TOUGH TIMES, FEED THEM!

If they have to come in on a weekend, or stay late, bring donuts. Buy pizza. *(Include a fruit salad for us health-nuts!)* Or, if the team is getting down, suggest a potluck long lunch where the team can take a break, chat about topics other than this infernal change. Offer fun prizes periodically of $5 coffee shop gift cards or free lunch at the office café. Have a stress-busting candy jar on your desk making you a little more accessible *(and delicious)*. Working remotely? No problem! Have a surprise snack/meal delivered. It's a fun and easy way to say "Thank you"; "We're in this together"; "You got this, Boo"; or "At least we won't starve" when things are at their most frustrating.

## PLEASE NOTE:

This is not the only positive things you're doing, but in addition to communication, appreciation and trust building activities, this is a really nice touch."

# Tip #44

# CELEBRATE
# PROGRESS

Everyone plans a big celebration at the end, but with a change that takes months/ years to execute, consider a celebration of progress!

# BUILD IN MILESTONE CELEBRATIONS BECAUSE WHEN YOU'RE CHARGING TOWARDS THE LIGHTHOUSE THAT'S MILES AWAY, IT'S NICE TO STOP, LOOK BACK, AND SEE HOW FAR YOU'VE COME.

It's a quick and easy time for appreciation and acknowledgment of effort, even if things haven't been going exactly to plan…ESPECIALLY if things haven't been going exactly to plan! Your team is going to be deflated by the lack of perfect success, so be sure to keep them charged up by pointing out what DID go right and discussing the ways the team can continue their progress forward.

HAVING AN ACTION PLAN FOR IMPROVEMENT WILL HELP PEOPLE SHIFT THEIR FOCUS FROM "WOE IS US" TO "WE'VE GOT THIS."

# TIP #45

## GENUINELY
# THANK THEM

*I SAID IT IN TIP #25: APPRECIATE APPRECIATE APPRECIATE!; AND I'LL SAY IT AGAIN.*

## BE SURE YOU'RE APPRECIATING THE EFFORT THAT YOUR TEAM IS PUTTING OUT THERE.

Pay special attention to making sure that your resisters and other more-prickly folks feel it. It's easy to say "thanks" and "nice job" to your rock stars. One of the best ways to turn resisters into acceptors is to make them feel seen, heard, appreciated, and valued. It takes a lot of emotional intelligence and patience on the part of the leader, but your extra effort is an investment in a massive commitment from someone on your team with serious untapped potential!

*THINK ABOUT IT THAT WAY FOR A CHANGE!*

# Tip #46

## CREATE OUTLET
### FOR
# APPRECIATING
## EACH OTHER

Ok, so it's all good and fun if you're running around thanking everyone and appreciating their hard work and value, but you're just one little leader. How can you exponentially increase the impact of appreciation?

## GET THE WHOLE TEAM IN ON THE ACTION!

I was walking back to the training room at a medical facility one time, and we passed a massive bulletin board with a huge picture of Chuck Norris doing a side kick. About a billion post-its were stuck to the board. I asked what it was, and the HR director proudly said, "It's our Chuck Norris Kick Butt Board!" He proceeded to explain that any time anyone did anything helpful, from holding the door when someone had their hands full, to taking over the Board of Director Presentation when someone else was sick, they could write it on a post-it and stick it on the board. She said that at first only the managers and supervisors put up post-its, but as soon as people experienced how good it felt to see their names up there, they all joined in. She said it changed the whole culture of the place. Instead of looking for how fellow co-workers were doing badly, they started looking for the good stuff. It was a game changer for them, and it can be for you, too!

THINK ABOUT HOW YOU CAN GET YOUR TEAM IN ON
MOTIVATING AND APPRECIATING EACH OTHER.

# TIP #47

## CAN YOU
# MAKE LIFE
## A LITTLE
## *EASIER?*

During the trek to the new comfort zone, people feel stretched, challenged, and often overworked. Finding a way you can reduce their burden during this time will make people feel appreciated and help them deal with the additional stress brought on by the change. Can you get a little extra help for them? Maybe temporarily lower the goals while they settle into the change. Or can you extend a few deadlines? Even though this may slow down business for a short time, it will give your team a little more capacity to innovate, and it will show that you're invested in their success. It'll also show that you understand the challenges that come with change, and appreciate the effort they're putting in.

## THAT SHOW OF SUPPORT WILL NEVER GO UNNOTICED.

Be clear what can't let up *(i.e. customer experience)* but give them a break if you can with an understanding of how long that break will last.

*That investment in their adjustment will pay dividends when it's time to crank back into full gear!*

# FLEXIBILITY

## AIN'T JUST FOR
YOGIS

# WHEN YOU'RE IN THE QUAGMIRE OF CHANGE, OFFER SOME KIND OF FLEXIBILITY...

...whether it's jeans on Friday, a flexible work schedule, Taco Tuesday, work from home option, or some other concession. Sometimes we have rules that are just the way it's always been but aren't necessary; if we can ease the norm in some way, people feel like the workplace is being customized to their needs. Of course, you're not going to give flexibility if it negatively impacts the job (you can't really offer a flexible work schedule for shift work), and you're going to clarify the guidelines around maintaining the flexibility (work from home once a week is fine as long as key metrics are maintained).

WITH CLARITY AND APPROPRIATE ALLOWANCE, YOUR TEAM WILL FEEL VALUED AS INDIVIDUALS, RATHER THAN JUST ANOTHER BEE IN THE HIVE.

# Tip #49

# FRANKEN-TROPHIES
## FOR THE
# WIN

PAGE 98

Sure, Employee of the Month, Top Salesperson, and Production Master are all vital awards and motivators to increase productivity and key performance indicators. But King of Cookies, Jester of Jokes, and Most Organized Office Supplies will lighten the daily pace, bring attention to fun pride points for the individuals on your team, and just generally improve the morale of the group.

CONSIDER SOME KIND OF SILLY ACKNOWLEDGMENT OF THE PEOPLE ON YOUR TEAM. IT DOESN'T HAVE TO BE SERIOUS ALL THE TIME.

In fact, creating a healthy outlet for fun will make people more committed during crunch time, and they'll have a stronger bond and trust between each other, which will help them get through the tough times.

## LIGHTEN UP, LORRAINE!

# TIP #50

## FIGHT FOR
## SUPPORT
### FOR THEM

When a team is dealing with change, it's important for team members to feel like their leader "has our backs" and is committed to helping them do their jobs as well as they can.

## WHEN YOUR TEAM NEEDS SOMETHING OR ASKS FOR SOMETHING, GO TO BAT FOR THEM.

Make a case and have the courage to fight for an additional support person during the change, or more training, additional equipment, or just higher-up acknowledgment of their efforts. When things don't go right, and your team is under fire, be sure you're standing behind their hard work and commitment wherever it's appropriate. When the team knows their leader is backing them up to upper management, less of an "us versus them" culture results.

*When you are able to get what they need, they'll feel supported.*

If you're not able, be sure you don't disparage the upper management or question their decision. Ask for the reason they're not able to provide what has been asked for so you can explain it to your team. Your team will probably still not like it, but if they can understand the business reason for it, they're more likely to be satisfied with not getting what they want.

# Tip #51

## FREQUENTLY

### ASK

# "HOW'S IT GOING?"

The second question you should be asking your people after telling them how much you appreciate them is "how it's going?" Certain people will be completely forth-right, and you won't need to pry it out of them, but some people won't be as open with you unless you ask.

## MAKE A POINT OF PERIODICALLY SEEKING OUT THOSE QUIETER PEOPLE ON YOUR TEAM.

### ASK HOW THEY'RE DOING.

Ask if they see any areas for improvement. Ask if they've come across any challenges that might help you guide the team. Involve them in the success of the project, and they'll feel more team pride, and more ownership in the success of the change.

# TIP #52

## FREQUENTLY
### ASK FOR THEIR
# INNOVATIONS

# EVERY TEAM HAS ITS ROCK STARS.

Whether their personality makes them naturally more open to change, or they have a built-in skillset that makes them good at this particular change, some people grab it and run with it, immediately making it work. Don't you love them? Be sure to engage these people in a conversation around what they're doing to be successful. They may have some insights that can help the resisters. You might even pair a resister with a rock star. Perhaps the rock star can explain something in a way you can't that will make the resister see it in a more positive light. Involve these "make it happen" Mavens in the success of the whole team and be sure to share specifically why you appreciate their particular brand of "Let's do this."

*You DEFINITELY WANT THOSE PEOPLE TO CONTINUE WHAT THEY'RE DOING!*

# TIP #53

## CRUSH THE CLIQUES

During the slog to our new comfort zone, the propensity to cliquify goes up! People get together with the people they like and relate to and vilify the resisters or the "goodie-two-shoe" rock stars. When gossip rages or conflict goes unaddressed, bring the whole team together and have a "rumor meeting" where you bring to light anything people have questions or unhealthy curiosities about *(in a welcoming, not a blaming, kind of way!).*

## CREATE UNLIKELY PARTNERSHIPS ON SMALLER PROJECTS TO BRING CERTAIN PEOPLE CLOSER.

HAVE TEAM BUILDING OR SKILL-BUILDING LUNCH-AND-LEARNS TO BRING INDIVIDUALS TOGETHER WHO MIGHT NOT OTHERWISE NORMALLY BOND.

*(Remember Tip #41: FEED THEM!)* The more people separate themselves, the more conflicts fester, so figure out ways to make them interact and talk. They'll roll their eyes at your "get to know you" games, but at the end of the day, they will come together. When you're working remotely, facilitating these interactions needs to be even more intentional, so get creative and make it happen.

# Tip #54

## TELL YOUR
## BOSS,
### AND THEIR BOSS!

# TAKE THE BLAME AND SHARE THE GLORY!

A great leader understands that the success of the whole team reflects on their excellence. In other words, don't be hoggin' the crown! If someone in the C-suite points out what a great job you're doing, thank them and acknowledge the massive efforts of your team to make it happen during the tough times. When someone on your team does something exceptional, tell someone in upper management about it, and ask them to write a note to that team member, or stop by and thank them.

BE SURE YOU'RE GLORIFYING YOUR WHOLE TEAM, BECAUSE THAT WILL MAKE THEM FEEL VALUED, GIVE THEM TEAM PRIDE, AND THEY'RE LIKELY TO DOUBLE THEIR EFFORTS TOWARDS PROJECT SUCCESS AS A RESULT.

## WHO WOULDN'T WANT THAT?

# TIP #55

## KEEP GOAL
# ACHIEVEMENT
## IN THEIR FACE

Ya know those thermometer things that fund-raisers use to help illustrate the progress towards the monetary goal? I like using visuals like that to illustrate progress towards a big team goal, too! Instead of coloring in the dollar amounts, put the progressive milestones on there, and make a production of filling it in once achieved. Or maybe it's something that's ceremoniously ripped down once completed. Whatever it is, it will help your team see how far they've come. *(See Tip #29: Be positive, but not too much!!)*

## FROM THAT VISUAL REMINDER OF PROGRESS, YOU HAVE OUTLINED THE MILESTONES, SO YOUR TEAM DOESN'T HAVE TO THINK ABOUT THE HUGE CHANGE AHEAD.

*They just have to think of getting to that next step.*

# FUN GAMES
## TO GET THROUGH THE
### YUCKY STUFF

The first time someone told me about Office Chair Olympics, I thought, "What a terrible idea!" But the spirit of it was to take 15 minutes, have a stupid competition, laugh, reduce stress, have some fun, then get back to the stressful hard work. Imagine a chili tasting competition to release positive endorphins and crown the Chili Monarch, or a paperclip-flipping contest to see who can get closest to the target, or a naming challenge for the new office mascot fichus tree.

HAVE SOME FUN FOR CRYING OUT LOUD.
LOOSEN YOUR BONNET AND HAVE A LAUGH.

# OBVIOUSLY, WE LIMIT IT AND DON'T LET IT GET IN THE WAY OF PRODUCTIVITY, BUT IT'S AMAZING HOW A 15-MINUTE LAUGH BREAK CAN RE-FOCUS PEOPLE ONCE IT'S OVER.

*(Be sure to announce the time beforehand so those who don't like to be interrupted will know it's coming.)*

BONUS

# FINAL

## WORDS

*Well, that's it!*

# REMEMBER, CHANGE IS HARD.

Not only are you trying to lead others through change, you've also got to deal with it yourself, so don't forget to give yourself a break, drink plenty of water, and find your own escape outside of work. That way, you'll have the emotional energy to deal with other people's challenges when they need you.

# ANNE BONNEY

IS A FUN, ENERGETIC INTERNATIONAL MOTIVATIONAL KEYNOTE SPEAKER AND INFLUENCE IGNITOR

She is an authority on change, author of **GET OVER IT!**, podcast host of *Ignite Your Influence Podcast* , and an experienced leadership workshop and retreat facilitator in leadership, emotional intelligence and effective communication. Her workshops, keynotes and retreats produce valuable shifts in thinking and behavior, and they're a ton of fun!

After 20 years in highly successful corporate and non-profit leadership positions, Anne, now uses her experience, education, and expertise to ignite your ability to influence others by harnessing emotional intelligence, courageously communicating and effectively dealing with change.

You'd better turn on the AC because this "ball of fire" will light you up with fun and relevant stories, time-tested knowledge and immediately applicable strategies to make a difference for you, your team, and your organization.

This spunky little redhead shares business lessons from her crazy life experiences, which arms her with relatable and hilariously memorable stories from growing up overseas, running international marathons, animal training, morale building tours to the military in Iraq, volunteering at an elephant sanctuary and singing opera at a performing arts school and yes- there's more. Anne is a mindset shifting motivator who fires people up to catalyze powerful change in their lives, their teams and their organizations.

**www.YourChangeSpeaker.com | Anne@AnneBonney.com**
**PODCAST:** https://igniteyourinfluence.buzzsprout.com/
(OR FIND IT ON YOUR FAVORITE PODCAST CHANNEL)

CPSIA information can be obtained
at www.ICGtesting.com
Printed in the USA
LVHW101531180821
695282LV00001B/4